Handbook
for
Today's
Parish Leaders

Handbook
for
Today's
Parish Leaders

- *Responding to the call to lead*

- *Collaboration, communion, and community*

- *Practical ways to develop leadership skills*

GINGER INFANTINO

Liguori
ONE LIGUORI DRIVE
LIGUORI MO 63057-9999

Imprimi Potest:
Harry Grile, CSsR, Provincial
Denver Province, The Redemptorists

Published by Liguori Publications
Liguori, Missouri 63057

To order, call 800-325-9521
www.liguori.org

Library of Congress Cataloging-in-Publication Data
Infantino, Ginger.
  Handbook for today's parish leader / Ginger Infantino.
     p. cm.
  Includes bibliographical references.
  ISBN 978-0-7648-2001-4
  1. Lay ministry--Catholic Church. I. Title.
  BX1920.I54 2011
  253--dc23
                                2011023409

Liguori Publications, a nonprofit corporation, is an apostolate of the Redemptorists. To learn more about the Redemptorists, visit Redemptorists.com.

Printed in the United States of America
15 14 13 12 11 / 5 4 3 2 1
First Edition

CONTENTS

ACKNOWLEDGMENTS

This handbook is dedicated to Fr. Bob Wild, who saw leadership qualities in me that I didn't see in myself, and to Sr. Therese Kinsel, who nourished my fledgling attempts at being a leader. I treasure the love and support of my husband, Bob, who has journeyed with me and encouraged my ministry every step of the way. He is a true Christian leader, an inspiration, and a witness. I am truly grateful for Bob's exceptional editorial talents as he diligently proofread and made suggestions for this book.

I am thankful to our children—Bob, Susan, Debbie, Karen, Amy, and Paul—who demonstrate active Christian leadership in the midst of tremendously busy lives. Their love, dedication, and commitment (and that of their spouses and children) give me hope for our Church.

Many thanks to my sisters in faith—Georgia, Sandy, Sharon, Judy, and Yolanda—who pray and share spirituality with me each week and help me to mature in my faith.

I am deeply appreciative to Liguori Publications, especially to Fr. Mat Kessler and Fr. Scott Katzenberger, for giving me this opportunity to share my experience as a leader, and to Pamela Brown, who affirms and supports my publications and workshops with such enthusiasm.

Finally, I give thanks and praise to God for all the leaders of our Church—laypeople, ordained, and religious—who carry out on the mission and ministry of Jesus Christ in the twenty-first century. I pray that this book will strengthen and assist them in some small way as they respond to their call to follow Jesus as a leader.

SECTION ONE

THE CALL TO LEAD

This handbook is for everyone—people already established in parish-leadership positions, people who are new to parish leadership, and people who aren't sure whether they are called to be leaders. This section presents background information and ways for you to continue processing the ideas in each chapter on your own.

1

REFLECTIONS OF AN
UNQUALIFIED LAY PERSON (ULP)

God's story in each of our lives is unique and distinctive. It's a one-of-a-kind "bestseller" written in our hearts with people, experiences, traditions, happy and sad times, hurts and healings, and more than a few miracles. I sometimes jokingly say that I'm a wonderful Christian—in retrospect. When I look back over my life, I see all the ways God is present. I become aware of how God brought seemingly insignificant or unconnected events together to work for good in my life. I see how even painful experiences were points of growth and helped me to trust and mature in my faith.

Even though everyone's story is unique, when we share our stories we find they are laced with common threads. I'm sharing a bit of my story to show that if we are willing, God will use us as instruments. If we are willing, God can fashion even a quiet, shy, rather introverted young woman into a leader.

In the late sixties, our parish in Buffalo, New York, was very blessed to have an associate pastor who took the directives of the Second Vatican Council to heart. Fr. Bob invited interested parishioners to study the documents of Vatican II. After several weeks, he asked us to select an area of interest mentioned in the documents.

Parishioners formed small groups—such as Catholic education, religious education, social ministry, liturgy, and finances—to implement these elements into our parish life. The chairpersons of these groups formed our first parish council.

My husband, a teacher, selected Catholic education; I chose preschool religious education. We had four children under age seven, and I was expecting our fifth, so preschool religion was a natural choice. Besides, with my low self-esteem I felt there wasn't too much I could do to mess up preschoolers.

As often happens, when you express an interest in something, you're put in charge of it. I was asked to form a committee to initiate a preschool religion program for three- to five-year-olds. Fr. Bob insisted that everyone be trained for his or her responsibilities, so I took a preschool-catechist formation course taught by Christiane Brusselmans, a leading catechist and liturgist. Like a thirsty sponge, I absorbed every word and came back to the parish brimming with enthusiasm.

That autumn we began our first preschool program. My own religion came alive as I served as preschool coordinator and catechist. I relearned beautiful concepts in the language of preschoolers—I am loved by God, I am called and gifted, I am chosen in my baptism to be holy and do God's work. Somehow, in all my time in Catholic education (grade one through freshman year in college), I had learned all those concepts only with my head. Now, for the first time, I was learning them with my heart.

A few years later, when Fr. Bob accepted a new ministry, he suggested to our pastor that I take over his responsibilities for all religious education in the parish. I was not sure about taking such a great responsibility, but he asked me to consider three things: Would I be willing to study and learn? Would I endeavor to pray and deepen my own spirituality? Would I commit my time, aside from my family responsibilities, to the religious education of the parish?

With God's help, I said yes, a yes that set me on an incredible life journey. I became the first lay religious-education director at our parish.

When our parochial-school principal, a dedicated and committed woman religious, heard of my appointment, she was incredulous. She politely told me that I should not hold that position because I was only an Unqualified Lay Person. I teased my husband, who was completing his doctorate: He would have EdD after his name, and I would have ULP after mine.

Of course, in many ways our principal was correct. I had little academic qualification or experience for this position, but in my heart I knew I was being called by God to do this new thing called religious-education director. The Holy Spirit was leading me to pray, to study, and to learn. I was being asked to use my gifts for coordination, organization, and practicality and to put them at the service of the Lord.

For several years, I worked with our priests and many dedicated laypeople to yield a vibrant religious-education program for preschoolers through adults. We developed a very successful adult spiritual-renewal program called Mission that touched the hearts of our parishioners and spread to other parishes. I felt extremely fulfilled as a Catholic woman, wife, and mother. And then my husband accepted a position as assistant professor of education at the University of San Diego.

Even though I had very mixed emotions about moving

across the country and leaving our extended families and our beautiful parish community, God provided many signs to encourage me to say yes again. We moved to San Diego, and many tears later I was blessed with the opportunity to go to the university as a rather old sophomore. I completed an undergraduate degree in religious studies and master's degree in religious education and was offered a position with the Diocesan Office for Evangelization and Catechetical Ministry.

With my degrees and lengthy experience (forty-plus years in catechetical ministry), I am finally qualified in the eyes of most. However, I also am very aware that the Lord called me to ministry when I was unqualified in the eyes of many. God called me to be a leader through an associate pastor who saw something in me that I didn't see in myself.

This is how many people are called to lead in the Church today. They may or may not have an academic degree in theology, they may or may not have lengthy experience, and they may or may not have many family or work obligations, but they are still willing to put their gifts at the service of the Church.

I could never have imagined where that first yes would take me. The young wife and mother of five who was unqualified but said yes anyway has become an old wife, mother of six, and grandmother of nine who, with God's grace, was able to fulfill her potential to be all that God was calling her to be. Our family is spread from Virginia to California to Hawaii, but all are Christian leaders, whether in music, choir, catechesis, adult formation, social-ministry outreach, or Catholic-school education.

Even though I'm retired, God isn't finished with me yet; I still have more yeses to give. But for all I've experienced, I have only gratitude in my heart. My life as a Church leader is blessed with grace in abundance. So many outstanding people, so many wonderful experiences, so much learning, and so many challenges have shaped me and helped me grow. Leadership in the Church isn't always easy, but it's always full of meaning.

Practical Suggestions for Individuals

◆ Consider journaling several times a week. Use a small notebook you can carry with you. Write in it as the Spirit moves you, and be sure to date each entry.

◆ Choose a quiet time and space. Think about your own bestseller—*God's Story in My Life*. What people, events, and experiences will you include in your unique narrative? Record some of these thoughts in your journal now.

Practical Suggestions for Parish Groups

◆ Parish councils, the parish staff, committees, or specific ministry groups (lectors, catechists, service groups) may want to use this book as a discussion tool for a portion of their meetings. If members of the group have not yet done so, participants can briefly share how they became involved in their current ministry. The group may want to review and discuss one of the recent Church documents suggested in chapters 2 through 4.

2

FOLLOW THE LEADER

A beautiful and challenging contemporary religious song called "The Summons" asks whether we will follow Jesus if he calls our name. This inspirational piece, with lyrics by John Bell, precisely captures the call of every baptized Christian—we are called by name to follow Jesus Christ and never be the same. This invitation or summons to be a follower of Jesus is offered to each of us through baptism.

In the Gospels, this summons is extended in various ways. The angel invites the young Mary to give birth to the one who will change the world forever (Luke 1:26–38). Jesus beckons Levi, the tax collector, with two simple words, "Follow me" (Matthew 9:9). Peter is called to set out into deep waters and lower his nets for a catch; from now on, he will catch people (Luke 5:4–10). The healed demoniac is asked to follow Jesus by going home to his family and proclaiming what the Lord has done (Mark 5:19–20). During his public ministry, Jesus lovingly invites ordinary people to be his followers: sometimes in word, sometimes by touch, sometimes through a healing or miracle. The lives of these ordinary people are transformed forever, and they become disciples.

The disciples called by Jesus clearly emerge as leaders. They follow Jesus, listen to his teaching, and are sent to do the same things Jesus does. A closer examination of the Gospels yields other courageous but nameless leaders: the young boy who comes forth from the 5,000 and offers his five loaves and two fish to feed the multitude (John 6:9); the woman at the well who proclaims to her town in Samaria that she has found the Messiah (John 4:39); and the bold woman who crashes a dinner party and anoints Jesus for his burial (Mark 14:8–9). In Acts of the Apostles, we learn of early Church members who gave all their belongings and lived in community, ensuring that no one was needy (2:42–47). In the Epistles, we discover countless leaders who opened their homes, hosted the eucharistic meal, and financially supported the mission of the blossoming Church.

The summons to follow Jesus extended over two millennia ago continues to be offered to us. When we accept the invitation, an interesting paradox and unique occurrence transpires. When we become followers of Jesus we, the *followers*, grow to become the *leaders* just as it happened over two thousand years ago.

In calling us to be his disciples, Jesus invites us to leadership—in our families, in our church, in our work, in our society. This notion of being a leader may frighten us a bit; perhaps we don't envision ourselves as having a leadership role in *any* areas. We may not consider ourselves leaders in our family if we're not parents or guardians. We may not think of ourselves as parish leaders if we're not parish staff members or ministry coordinators. We may shun the idea of being a leader in our work environment or society because we aren't in charge of any group. However, in considering how to respond to Jesus' summons, we may need to broaden our concept of what leadership means. We may need to pay closer attention to the ways Jesus leads.

Clearly, Jesus is a leader who meets the popular understanding of what that term means. Jesus selects and manages a group of people he sees as having the potential to continue his mission, even though they probably are not the people *we* would select. He holds regular meetings with them. He teaches and mentors them for three years so they understand his vision even though they seem to consistently misunderstand what he is about. Finally, he commissions this ragtag group of disciples to carry on his mission even though they are afraid, will deny him, and will abandon him in his last hour.

Jesus, the Servant Leader

The image of leadership that Jesus models, however, goes well beyond the popular understanding of the term. Through word, action, and example, Jesus captures and clarifies his vision of the true leader: the greatest is the least (Luke 9:48), the last are first (Matthew 19:30), the lost are sought (Luke 19:10). This "least, last, lost" mentality turns most of our ideas of leadership inside out. Scripture gives a clear picture of Jesus the Servant Leader, who

+ ministers to the needs of others,

+ empowers the powerless,

+ mentors the inexperienced,

+ walks with the troubled,

+ serves the underserved,

+ shares resources with people who are lacking,

- ✛ encourages the downhearted,
- ✛ heals the hurting,
- ✛ preaches the Good News,
- ✛ responds to peoples' needs without counting the cost,
- ✛ witnesses to the mercy and compassionate love of God,
- ✛ listens and explains what is not understood,
- ✛ challenges the hypocritical,
- ✛ fosters a divine relationship through personal prayer and reflection, and
- ✛ inspires and touches hearts and lives.

When we scrutinize the manner in which Jesus leads, we deepen our understanding of what leadership means for contemporary Christians. Our vision is clarified, and we see new possibilities to lead—in our families, our parish communities, our work environments, and our society. Striving to pattern our lives on the principles and ideals of Jesus, we uncover numerous opportunities where we too can be servant leaders.

Our Call to Be Servant Leaders

Laypeople of the twenty-first century are summoned to serve in many pressing ways in the environments in which we live, work, and socialize. The Second Vatican Council's Dogmatic Constitution on the Church notes that laypeople have a mission to evangelize their environments (33). A paraphrasing of Saint Teresa of Ávila's prayer puts this mission succinctly: Christ has no body now but ours. Christ uses our eyes to look with compassion on the Earth and our hands and feet to do good and bless others.

Parish communities are in critical need of lay leaders, a need not precipitated by any crisis in the priesthood or lack of religious vocations. The importance and necessity of lay leadership is occurring as the Church clarifies its understanding of dynamic ways to carry out the mission of Christ in today's culture. The Church is deepening its comprehension of the role and responsibility of the laity. Pope Benedict reinforced this maturing understanding when he said that laypeople are not simply collaborators with the clergy but share responsibility for the Church (May 26, 2009, and March 7, 2010). In the decades since Vatican II, parish communities have been animated by thousands of lay leaders who, under the direction of their pastors, fulfill an important leadership role in the Church.

In many parishes, lay staff are responsible for ministries involving liturgy, catechetics, social issues, youth, schools, and Rite of Christian Initiation of Adults (RCIA). Laypeople coordinate programs for lectors, extraordinary ministers of holy Communion, altar servers, food pantries, home visitation, and evangelization. Laypeople also serve in high-level positions in most dioceses.

Many parishes foster a variety of opportunities for lay leaders to help meet the needs of their brothers and sisters. These leaders don't have designated ministries in the Church like lector, liturgist, or catechist. They are, nonetheless, servant leaders among their peers. They are willing to help others at a particular time or in a particular situation—for instance, cancer survivors willing to walk with others going through chemotherapy, people who send birthday cards in the name of the parish to homebound people, people who make sandwiches for those with AIDS, and people who have experienced the ravages of addiction or abuse who are willing to talk to others in the same situation. When a community has fires, floods, or other disasters, the parish staff counts on help from laypeople of all ages.

When leadership is equated to service, each parish has a way for every parishioner to lead. Each person has a responsibility to find his or her way to serve. Opportunities become available to people of all ages, stages, abilities, intellectual capacities, social status, language, and ethnic and cultural backgrounds. The possibilities for leadership are limited only by a person's lack of desire, initiative, energy, or strength to follow the call.

When we begin to see that true leadership involves serving the needs of others the way Jesus did, we accept the summons to follow Jesus wherever he leads. We are motivated to leave the ranks of "pew potato" and joyfully accept our responsibility as members of the Church. We discard the pay, pray, and obey mentality and actively embrace our role as servant leaders. Instead of viewing church as someplace we go to receive something each week, we understand that we are an integral part of the parish community, a community of interdependent members of the Body of Christ.

Practical Suggestions for Individuals

◆ Download contemporary commissioning or call songs such as "The Summons," (John Bell; GIA Publications); "You Are Mine," (David Haas; GIA); "Servant Song" (Donna Marie McGargill, OSM; OCP); "St. Theresa's Prayer" (John Michael Talbot, Birdwing Music/EMI); "*Vayan Al Mundo* (Go Out to the World)" (Jaime Cortez, OCP).

◆ Read stories of call in the Gospels: Luke 1:26–38, Matthew 9:9, Luke 5:4–11, Mark 5:1–20. Meditate on these challenging songs and Gospel texts. Use them for prayer, keeping in mind that the invitation to discipleship is being extended to you.

◆ In what areas is the Lord calling you to a new or deeper commitment? Where can you be instrumental in bringing the loving, healing, forgiving touch of Christ? Record your answers in your journal and pray about them.

◆ If you were born after Vatican II, talk with a family member or parishioner who experienced the changes involving the laity.

Practical Suggestions for Parish Groups

◆ Study the Vatican II documents Dogmatic Constitution on the Church (*Lumen Gentium*) and Decree on the Apostolate of the Laity (*Apostolicam Actuositatem*). Note the calls to greater lay leadership.

◆ In small groups, discuss how your parish has integrated the major concepts of these documents. These discussions will be enhanced if your parish priests and staff participate.

◆ Discuss three to five areas, such as social justice or right-to-life ministries, in which your parish could continue to expand in its understanding of the roles of laypeople.

3

THEOLOGICAL CONSIDERATIONS FOR LAY LEADERS

Several theological principles shape and influence our ministry as lay leaders. When these considerations are integrated into our life perspective, they provide understanding, direction and a spiritual underpinning for spirituality and ministry.

God's Everlasting Love

Our awesome and magnificent God loves each of us into existence; God knew us before we were born, knitting us in our mother's womb (Psalm 139). Created in God's own image and likeness (Genesis 1:27), we are graced with God's everlasting presence and unconditional love (Jeremiah 31:3). This love is pure gift and grace, freely given—not dependent on our intelligence, ability, status, success, attitude, or even behavior. This outpouring of love is manifested in creation, in covenant, in the Law, in the Scriptures, and in other created beings.

We see and experience this immeasurable and abundant love of God most completely in the person of Jesus Christ, whom God sent to save us. Jesus discloses God's limitless love to us through his teachings, his parables, healings, miracles, and works. By his life, death, and resurrection, Jesus reveals the unconditional love of God and demonstrates God's great mercy, rich compassion, and generous forgiveness. Jesus sends his Spirit to help us live in response to God's love.

Our Response to God's Love

It may be difficult to understand the depth and breadth of God's unconditional and never-ending love, but as we begin to appreciate our status as graced beings, our response can only be one of praise and thanksgiving. As Christians, once we acknowledge the place of God's grace in our lives, we want to know God more intimately, to accept Jesus as our Savior and Lord, and to allow the Holy Spirit to work. We rely on the gifts of the Spirit to help us live a Christ-centered life serving others.

When we examine our lives and find God, when we are surrounded by God's beauty and goodness in others and in creation, and when we uncover God's presence even (or most especially) in our dark and difficult times, we are filled to overflowing with a gratitude we express by living a life worthy of our calling (Ephesians 4:1) and by allowing the gifts and blessings of creation to lead us to a deeper relationship with the Creator.

Baptism Empowers Us

Baptism, the first sacrament of initiation and the gateway to the other sacraments, forms and configures us to Christ (*Catechism of the Catholic Church*, 1272). It cleanses all sin, invites us to holiness and discipleship, and calls us to participate in the ministry and mission of Christ as members of the Church (1279). Indelibly marked for Christ, we receive baptism only once. However, the graces of our baptism are poured out continuously and celebrated throughout our lives, empowering us to live and serve as committed Christians.

The sacraments of initiation—baptism, confirmation, and Eucharist—call us, strengthen us, and nourish us to live discipled lives as members of the community called the Church. As members of that community, we are "a chosen race, a royal priesthood, a holy nation, a people of his own, so that you may announce the praises" (1 Peter 2:9). The grace of the sacraments allows us to grow into the disciples we are called to be.

Ordination Presumes Ministry

As laypeople, our call to be disciples and to serve as leaders is rooted and grounded not in the sacrament of holy orders, but in the sacrament of baptism. We are "'anointed' by the Holy Spirit, incorporated into Christ who is anointed priest, prophet, and king" (*CCC* 1241). By Baptism they share in the priesthood of Christ, in his prophetic and royal mission,…the common priesthood of all believers" (1268).

Through the sacrament of holy orders, priests "are consecrated in order to preach the Gospel and shepherd the faithful as well as to celebrate divine worship as true priests of the New Testament" (1564). Ordination presumes ministry, but ministry does not demand ordination. We assume that the ordained pastors will shepherd their parish communities and provide pastoral care and leadership (see *Code of Canon Law*, 519), but all Christians by virtue of their baptism have a responsibility to serve, to minister, and to lead as part of their own Christian vocation.

The ministries of the ordained and of laypeople are complementary—not competing—ministries. In an animated and vibrant parish community, laypeople and ordained collaborate to build up the body of Christ—all putting their gifts, talents and the sacramental grace proper to their vocation at the service of the Lord.

Continuing Jesus' Mission and Ministry

Our membership in the Church entails roles and responsibilities according to our status and our state in life. We're not simply volunteers who contribute to the mission when we have spare time. Discipleship is constituent with what it means to be Christian. The 1965 Vatican II Decree on the Apostolate of the Laity (*Apostolicam Actuositatem*) says that members who don't make their best effort to contribute to the growth of the Church are useless to the Church and to themselves (2). In subsequent passages, the Decree notes that laypeople, gifted with apostolic spirit and zeal, can draw others to the Church (especially those who have been away) and cooperate in the spread of the word of God. Nourished by the sacraments, laypeople are able to increase the effectiveness of pastoral care and assist in the administration of the Church's goods with expertise (10).

Laypeople are an integral part of the parish community; our perspective should always be viewed through the lens of discipleship. No matter what our status, vocational call, age, ethnic background, or gender, we are first and foremost disciples of Jesus Christ. As people actively involved in continuing Christ's ministry, we are called to active membership in our parish community.

Existing to Evangelize

The early Church enthusiastically carried out the mandate given by Jesus Christ as he ascended into heaven: "Go, therefore, and make disciples of all the nations, baptizing them in the name of the Father, and of the Son, and of the holy Spirit, teaching them to observe all that I have commanded you. And behold, I am with you always, until the end of the age" (Matthew 28:19–20). With certain urgency the disciples traveled to the ends of the known world, evangelizing, teaching, and proclaiming the saving message of Christ. Filled with the fire of the Holy Spirit and relying on the promise of the Lord's presence, these disciples spread the Good News, carried out the ministry of Jesus, baptized new disciples, and taught these neophytes as they themselves had been taught.

This missionary mandate and its promise extend to the Church today; they were bestowed on the Church as its foremost mission for all time. In his 1975 apostolic exhortation On Evangelization in the Modern World, Pope Paul VI affirmed that evangelization is the reason for the Church's existence (*Evangelii Nuntiandi*, 14).

To emphasize the importance of this document to the American Church, in 1992 the United States Conference of Catholic Bishops published *Go and Make Disciples: A National Plan and Strategy for Catholic Evangelization in the United States.* The plan heightens awareness of the evangelizing mission of the Church and sets specific goals for evangelization in the United States:

+ to instill in Catholics an enthusiasm for their faith so that they want to share it with others;

+ to proclaim the Good News about the saving message of Jesus and invite others to come into the fullness of the Catholic faith; and

+ to foster and promote Gospel values in our nation (27–33).

Evangelization is not the task of only the ordained, the vowed religious, or a few professional staff persons who are called to the specific ministry of evangelization. Evangelization is the responsibility of each member of the parish community. We are the only ones who can use our unique gifts to evangelize our particular environments; no one can do it exactly the way we can. As we evangelize our environments, we are assured and sustained by the promise that the Lord Jesus is present with us through his Holy Spirit.

Evangelization Is the Agenda

Evangelization is not another committee to be formed, department to be established, class to be taught, or program to be designed. It is not an agenda item for the parish council. Evangelization *is* the agenda. Each parish community must determine how it can integrate an evangelizing spirit into every aspect of parish life and how to place evangelization at the heart of its vision and direction.

For example, a parish should examine how welcome people feel when they call the parish or come for liturgy, how the parish responds to people who come for sacraments such as matrimony or baptism of their children after being away from Church life, and how parish members meet the needs of the alienated or underserved outside the parish.

Practical Suggestions for Individuals

◆ Cultivate an attitude of gratitude. List in your journal the gifts and blessings you've received. Include things you take for granted. Spend time in praise and thanksgiving each day. When you have an especially difficult time, go back and review your list.

◆ For thought or for your journal: Which of your environments—family, work, neighborhood, parish, or social—is in most need of evangelization? How will you bring the healing, forgiving, loving touch of Christ to that environment?

Practical Suggestions for Parish Groups

◆ The U.S. Bishops' book *Go and Make Disciples* (a free online full-text version is posted at usccb.org) has lists of practical goals (nos. 45–60), including fostering an experience of conversion and renewal and more active living of Catholic life, encouraging a deeper sense of prayer, making parishes more welcoming, helping Catholics feel comfortable about sharing their faith, and effectively inviting people to our Church. Parish staffs and councils could discuss these strategies and their application to their parishes. An extended discussion of this document, available in English and Spanish, can be a foundation for a parish vision statement with goals and strategies for evangelization.

4

MINISTERS
IN THE VINEYARD

In October 2010 thirty-three Chilean miners, trapped underground for more than sixty days, captured the world's attention. When they were rescued, most were wearing shirts that said, "¡Gracias Señor! Thank you Lord." For more than sixty days, this community of men grew in faith and hope in God as well as in unity and solidarity with each other. Each miner assumed a leadership role in some aspect of the survival process; if each didn't give his all to his task, the community wouldn't have functioned and perhaps wouldn't have survived.

The miners' story reminds us of Saint Paul's analogy of the body found in 1 Corinthians: "There are different kinds of spiritual gifts but the same Spirit; there are different forms of service but the same Lord" (12:4). Paul teaches that all parts of the body are needed for the body to function effectively (12:12–27).

The situation in a parish isn't as desperate as the Chilean miners'. But in many ways the survival of today's parishes may be in question if members of the Body of Christ don't embrace their role and responsibility as leaders.

Degrees of Responsibility

The scope of parish leadership reaches across a broad spectrum encompassing many roles and responsibilities. Parish leaders are ordained men, consecrated women and men, or laywomen and laymen. In most parishes, ordained priests serve the overall pastoral and administrative responsibilities. Parishes without a resident pastor are increasingly administered by religious or lay women and men. Nonordained people, who usually have advanced degrees in theology or pastoral ministry, oversee and coordinate daily parish and pastoral activities. An ordained priest is available to preside at the weekly Eucharist and to administer other sacraments. The nonordained parish ministers are known by various titles, including pastoral associate or parish coordinator.

Depending on the parish's size, number of parishioners, and cultural make-up, professional parish staff members usually direct catechetical, liturgical, Rite of Christian Initiation of Adults, school principal, Hispanic, youth, and social ministries. Since Vatican II, a remarkable number of women and men have served as professional lay ecclesial ministers.

Lay Ecclesial Ministers

In 1995, coinciding with the thirtieth anniversary of the Vatican II Decree on the Apostolate of the Laity (*Apostolicam Actuositatem*), the United States Conference of Catholic Bishops issued the statement "Called and Gifted for the Third Millennium." This document affirmed the gifts of the laity and used the term *ecclesial lay minister* to describe lay pastoral leaders in the Church. Ecclesial lay minister wasn't a new ministry, rank, or order in the Church; it encompassed a broad, generic category of lay professional ministers who collaborate closely with ordained ministers and who direct many parish programs.

Building on the foundation of "Called and Gifted," the bishops published guidelines for Lay Ecclesial Ministers in their 2005 book *Co-Workers in the Vineyard of the Lord: A Resource for Guiding the Development of Lay Ecclesial Ministry.* This book examines the theological foundations of lay ministry. It also gives guidelines for the spiritual, intellectual, psychological, and pastoral formation of lay ministers and offers suggestions for discerning a call to lay ecclesial ministry. While *Co-Workers* does not establish norms or laws regarding lay ministry, it does provide a "common frame of reference" as lay ministry continues to unfold in the United States. It recognizes lay ecclesial ministers as those whose roles require a "significant degree of preparation, formation, and professional competence" and "the authorization of the hierarchy in order for the person to serve publicly in the local church." These parish staff members are qualified to fulfill their ministry through advanced degrees or ministerial-formation programs in their specific ministries and through extensive ministerial experience.

Co-Workers encourages and offers support to the countless laypeople who assume ministerial and leadership roles in the Church. The bishops urge ordained and lay leaders to integrate lay ecclesial ministers into the life of the Church and suggest a need for a more thorough study of a theology of vocation.

Co-Workers sets out a positive, hopeful theology of lay ministry. It affirms not only lay ecclesial ministers, but encourages all laypeople to respond to their own personal call to lead and serve the Lord. "The same God who called Prisca and Aquila to work with Paul in the first century calls thousands of men and women to minister in our Church in this twenty-first century. This call is a cause for rejoicing."

Opportunities for Leadership

Even if one doesn't hold a professional ministerial role in the Church, the majority of Christians can find countless ways to exercise leadership roles as needs, concerns, projects, and opportunities arise. You may be invited by your pastor to lead a certain project. A parish staff member may seek you out because she sees qualities or gifts in you that you don't even see. You may respond to a notice in the parish bulletin or be inspired by some circumstance to serve. Perhaps a parish friend asks for help on a project.

You needn't be in high-profile positions to lead and serve. Stephen Covey, a noted writer on leadership, believes one needn't be in charge to be a leader. A person becomes a leader as soon as he or she begins influencing others.

Every parish needs its ordained ministers *and* its lay ecclesial ministers. A parish can effectively fulfill its mission only when a notable number of laypeople embrace their roles as leaders who can help in myriad ways:

+ Coordinators and workers in specific programs such as preschool, homebound visitation, social justice, parent groups in support of the parish school

+ Chairpersons and workers at yearly events like fund-raisers, blood drives, clothing drives

+ Liturgical ministers, including extraordinary ministers of holy Communion, lectors, greeters, choir members

+ Catechetical ministers, catechists, assistants

+ Facilitators and participants in Scripture study, small faith communities, prayer groups, bereavement groups

+ Weekly workers who count the collection, stuff parish bulletins, maintain parish facilities, assist in the parish office

+ Communications helpers who maintain the parish website and social-networking sites, assemble the parish newsletter, maintain the parish database, coordinate phone, text, or e-mail campaigns

As you accept your responsibility as parish leader, it may not be immediately clear where the path will lead. You may even be uncertain about the extent of what is being asked of you. What will be certain is that when you acknowledge your importance as a functioning member of the Body of Christ, you will be filled with great joy and peace, you will deepen your own spirituality, and you will mature as a Christian.

When the Chilean miners entered the mine, few understood what would be asked of them. But to survive, those miners became a community. Undoubtedly there were differences of opinion, fear, and questioning, but the bottom line was that each miner used his gifts for the benefit of all. What a fitting model for a discussion of leadership in the Church today.

Practical Suggestions for Individuals

◆ In your journal, list your skills and talents and the activities you enjoy. If you're uncertain about your gifts, ask friends or family.

◆ Look at your parish bulletin. Could your skills and talents be used in any of the activities? Take a first step by calling the person in charge and offering your help. If you see another way to contribute to the life of the parish, talk to your pastor or to a parish staff member.

Practical Suggestions for Parish Groups

◆ Discuss ways your parish can emphasize the work of lay ecclesial ministers and other parish leaders. During each month or season, highlight leaders from a different ministry: September, catechetical ministers; Advent, social ministers; January, Catholic-school personnel; Lent, liturgical ministers; June, ordained ministers. Be creative in letting the parish know how many people are really involved in a vibrant parish.

◆ Consider a ministry fair around Pentecost, the birthday of the Church, to encourage parishioners to become involved or reinvolved in parish life. Be sure that interested people are contacted in a timely manner. This *Handbook* would be a great gift for those who sign up.

5

WHAT YOU NEED TO KNOW

Parish leaders, especially compensated staff members and people coordinating major programs and events, need a foundation of basic information to be effective.

About the Parish

BASIC INFORMATION

+ Church mailing address, which may be different from the street address

+ Instructions for getting to the parish from all directions

+ Contact information: parish-office phone number(s), e-mail address, website and social-networking site URLs, phone numbers and e-mail addresses of parish ministers and/or staff

+ Parish-office hours and staff schedules

+ Parish publications, including bulletins, newsletters, websites, and social-networking sites

STATISTICS

+ Approximate number of parishioners and families in the parish

+ Age distribution: Knowing the number of children, teen, young-adult, middle-aged, and elderly parishioners will be helpful when scheduling and planning activities, classes, and other parish events

+ Marital status: percentages of single, married, widowed, and divorced parishioners

+ Educational and social status of parishioners, their ethnic and cultural make-up, and language groups

LEADERS

+ Pastor

+ Priests, deacons, parish administrators, and/or financial officers who help the pastor

+ Other professional staff members who minister at the direction of the pastor

+ The person who administers the parish office and activities, usually the parish secretary. (Many believe the parish secretary is one of the most influential people in the parish. She or he grants access to and schedules appointments with the pastor and has first-hand knowledge of most parish information and activities)

+ Parish-calendar administrator

+ Facility and/or maintenance coordinator

+ Person in charge of the parish bulletin, newsletter, website, social-working sites, and other communication tools

+ School principal and principal's assistant

FACILITIES

+ Method and forms for scheduling events

+ Procedures for opening and locking buildings

+ Process for having a room set up

+ Way to access lights, microphones, heat, and air-conditioning

+ Guidelines for using the kitchen, appliances, and utensils

+ Supplies you need to bring

+ Process for clean-up, including trash removal and rearrangement of the room after an event

EVENT COORDINATION

+ Approval process

+ Speaker guidelines

+ Publicity procedures

+ Financial-accountability rules

+ Program budgets

+ Expense processing

SAFETY AND SECURITY

+ Emergency procedures in case of fire, earthquake, tornado, or other disaster

+ Notification procedures in event of emergency

VISION STATEMENT

+ If your parish has a vision statement describing itself and its ministries, become familiar with it

+ If your parish doesn't have a vision statement, see Chapter 9 for information on developing one

About Your Ministry and Service

DIOCESAN AND PARISH POLICIES

+ Ask your pastor or immediate supervisor for the written policies or guidelines pertinent to your area of ministry or service

+ Give copies to your team members

YOUR JOB DESCRIPTION

+ You'll need a job description so you know what is expected of you and to whom you are responsible. It needn't be lengthy—it can be just the following information on an index card:

  - *Job title*
  - *Duties and responsibilities*
  - *Lines of communication*
  - *Length of commitment*

+ Compensated personnel should have a more formal, detailed job description

+ Leaders who work together should have a general understanding of each other's job descriptions. Know who does what—overlap can cause difficulties and misunderstandings

RESOURCES FOR PERSONAL AND MINISTERIAL GROWTH

+ Will the parish sponsor your attendance at workshops or courses?

+ What parish and diocesan resources (persons, print, media, and Internet) are available?

About Families

THE DOMESTIC CHURCH

+ *The family is the domestic Church.* The Second Vatican Council reemphasized this statement expressed originally by the early Church. The family is the primary and most basic community in which individuals are molded. Parents form their children in this first school of faith through example and by providing the foundation for belief, ethical behavior, and values.

+ All parents may not understand this call or may feel overwhelmed by this responsibility. The United States Conference of Catholic Bishops' 1994 statement "Follow the Way of Love" notes, "We need to enable families to recognize that they are a domestic church.... [A] family is holy not because it is perfect but because

God's grace is at work in it, helping it to set out anew every day on the way of love."

DIVERSE GROUPINGS

+ Many families fit the traditional nuclear-family model, but many do not. Households may include single young adults, multigenerational groupings, forever-families with adopted children, families headed by single parents, or blended families with his, her, and their children. Sometimes children in the same family have different last names. Adults may be in irregular marriages or living a lifestyle inconsistent with Church teaching. Families may be having economic insecurity, serious illness, divorce, separation, addiction or abuse.

+ As a parish leader it is important *not* to make judgments about family situations, but rather to extend the warm, hospitable outreach of the parish community. The simple task of registering people at an event may make you the first face of the Church to a person who is reticent about being there. Your welcoming acceptance or kind words may be the incentive for a person to return to the Church or to seek counseling or support.

CULTURE AND ETHNICITY

+ Your parish is a community of communities, of families with different ethnic and cultural backgrounds, practices, and traditions. The Church welcomes all the faithful, encouraging cultural identity while promoting unity through faith.

+ Learn about the traditions of the ethnic groups in your parish and respect the essential elements of each culture. Culturally sensitive leaders incorporate basic expressions of the culture and language where appropriate, such as including a Vietnamese hymn in a liturgical celebration or incorporating *Las Posadas* in a parish community where many people have Hispanic roots.

About Yourself

CONSIDER YOUR COMMITMENT

+ How much time and energy are you able to give to an undertaking?

+ Will you need to drop commitments to fulfill a new one?

+ Be aware of the built-in guilt factor. It's OK to say no. Be gracious in declining an invitation and leave the door open: "I can't be on that committee this spring, but consider me in the fall." "I can't pick up the donuts for parish hospitality every weekend, but I can do it one weekend a month."

+ Avoid being roped in for life. If there are no established terms, place your own time limit on your yes. This allows you to evaluate your continued service: "I'll facilitate the Scripture group this year, and then we can decide about the future."

+ Be up front with your colleagues and yourself about what you can do or cannot do: "I'm great at all the organizational details for the parish bazaar, but I'm not a good writer, so someone else needs to write the bulletin announcements and prepare the flyers."

Practical Suggestions for Individuals

◆ Keep important parish information in a folder or binder

◆ Place a reminder in your calendar to regularly visit your parish and diocesan websites

◆ Get a sense of the larger Church community by visiting the United States Conference of Catholic Bishops website (usccb.org) or the Vatican website (vatican.va)

Practical Suggestions for Parish Groups

◆ List the ways in which your parish is family-friendly. Brainstorm ways your parish can become more welcoming to families and young adults. Ask your youth-ministry group for input. How can you implement some of the suggestions?

◆ Discuss the major cultural groups in your parish. What cultural expressions can be highlighted in liturgy, catechesis, social events, your communication tools?

◆ Evaluate your parish communication tools. Are they appealing, up-to-date, and user-friendly? If not, get help from a tech-savvy parishioner.

6

SPIRITUALITY OF LAYPEOPLE

~

A water bearer in India walked to the river each day carrying two large pots suspended from a pole across his neck. One pot was perfect and always delivered a full portion of water for the master. The other pot was cracked and always arrived at the master's house half full. Naturally, the perfect pot was proud of its accomplishments. The cracked pot was ashamed that it could accomplish only half of its purpose.

One day the cracked pot said to the water bearer, "I'm ashamed. I leak water all the way back to the master's house. Because of my flaw, you don't get full value from your efforts even though you work hard."

The water bearer looked at the pot with compassion and said, "As we return to the master's house, I want you to notice the beautiful flowers along the path." And as they went up the hill, the cracked pot noticed the beautiful wild flowers on the side of the path, and this cheered it some.

The bearer said to the pot, "Did you notice the flowers are on your side of the path but not on the other side? That is because I used your imperfection. I planted flower seeds on your side of the path, and every day while we walk back from the river, you water them. For two years I have been able to pick these beautiful flowers to decorate the master's table. Without you being just the way you are, the master would not have this beauty to grace his house."

~

Christian life is a spiritual journey—a walk in which you are on your way to God while at the same time you are accompanied by God each step of the way. As you journey, you're increasingly aware of your own imperfections. You realize that all people are cracked pots—no one is perfect. You also grasp a very beautiful truth: God knows you, God loves you, and God will use you just the way you are—with your gifts, strengths, weaknesses, and imperfections. In spite of weakness or brokenness, God calls you be holy, to be sanctified, and to be set apart in order to serve.

The Christian Leader

As you mature in faith, you are invited to deeper holiness by developing and maintaining essential spiritual qualities and virtues. Your deepening faith life is expressed in the way you live, the witness you give, the rituals you participate in, and the service you offer. Certain spiritual qualities typify the Christian leader.

COMMITMENT TO CHRIST

Christian leaders are firmly committed to Jesus Christ as their Lord and Savior. Their decisions reflect that centrality. Christian leaders develop an intimate relationship with Christ through prayer, meditation, and reflection. The more they know Christ and his saving power, the more they love him. The more they love Christ, the greater their desire to follow him as disciples. The more they follow Christ, the stronger their ability to witness to him and bring others to Christ. With Saint Paul, the defining desire of Christian leaders is "to know him and the power of his resurrection" (Philippians 3:10).

In knowing, loving, and following Christ, leaders strengthen their relationship with the Trinity. Christ gently leads them to knowledge and understanding of God the Father and Creator, who loves them with an everlasting love, and to trust and have confidence in the power of the Holy Spirit, who inspires, corrects and animates them. With lives centered on Christ, leaders are grateful in the midst of success and joyful in the face of difficulty.

ESTEEM FOR THE SCRIPTURES

Seeking to know Jesus more intimately, to understand their Judeo-Christian heritage, and to learn about the ministry of the early Church, today's leaders treasure the Scriptures and reflect on them often. They understand that the Bible is the inspired Word of God written in the words of humans, and they invite this Word into their lives. Leaders believe in the power of the Word to form, inform, reform, and transform them. As the Word shapes their discipleship, they are motivated to share this powerful Word with others.

LOVE AND RESPECT FOR THE CHURCH

Christian leaders love and respect the Church inaugurated by Christ and his apostles. In a spirit of fidelity, they know the defining doctrines and teachings of the Church, are faithful to those teachings, and live a life consistent with them. They affirm the countless ways the Church extends Christ's healing, mercy, compassion, and justice to the weak, the poor, and the most vulnerable members of society, and they applaud the tremendous contribution the Church has made to human formation, growth, and potential through the centuries.

Leaders are saddened when scandal taints the reputation of the Church and undermines its good works, but they are aware that the Church, who calls all to ongoing conversion, is itself a wounded healer, a pilgrim Church in need of conversion.

ACTIVE PARTICIPATION IN THE LITURGY

Leaders are strengthened and supported in their ministry through the celebration of the sacraments, especially the Eucharist. They understand that Christ is alive and at work in his Church through the Eucharistic sacrifice, which is the "source and summit" of the Church's power and activity (Dogmatic Constitution on the Church [*Lumen Gentium*], 11). Leaders respond with full, conscious, and active participation.

Leaders are graced with rituals to celebrate initiation (baptism, confirmation, and Eucharist), healing (reconciliation and anointing), and vocation (matrimony and orders). These celebrations form them as one body, nourish them with Christ's body, and send them forth as discipled members of the Body of Christ. Their spirituality is enriched as they enter wholeheartedly into the liturgical seasons of Advent, Christmas, Lent, Easter, and Ordinary Time, and they are blessed and sustained by a Church that prays continuously through the Liturgy of the Hours.

DESIRE TO SERVE THE CHURCH

Leaders possess zeal and enthusiasm to serve Jesus Christ through service in the Church. Cultivating their involvement in the Church's mission, they practice the corporal and spiritual works of mercy and integrate beatitude living into their daily lives. Propelled by the Holy Spirit to evangelize, they preach the Good News through word, witness, hospitality, inclusion, and action.

VIRTUOUS LIVING

Lay leaders consistently strive to live a life of virtue and moral good. Realizing the joys and demands of this way of life, they are guided by the commands to love God above all and to love their neighbors as themselves, the Ten Commandments, and the precepts of the Church. They model their lives on holy and morally upstanding people: Mary, the Mother of God, the saints, and women and men who are contemporary witnesses. When they fall short and don't meet the demands of moral and virtuous living, leaders seek forgiveness and reconciliation.

Throughout life, God freely and abundantly bestows grace, a share in the divine life that enables and empowers Christians to act in love. Relying on this grace strengthens virtue and helps them to do good and avoid sin. Beginning at baptism, Christians are instilled with the theological virtues of faith, hope, and charity. Christian leaders strive to shape their conduct by practicing the foundational cardinal virtues of justice, prudence, temperance, and fortitude (*CCC* 1805–1809). Through repeated practice of virtue, leaders nurture their own upright living, grow in holiness, and serve as models for living life in Christ.

Ways to Deepen Spirituality

The Second Vatican Council reinforced the principle that regardless of one's state in life, all are called to holiness—laypeople, ordained, and women and men religious. Leaders respond to that call by taking steps to develop and maintain their spirituality.

MAKE TIME TO PRAY

Jesus often went away by himself to pray. It was prayer that animated the ministry of Jesus and sustained his relationship with his Father. It is prayer that will also animate your ministry and sustain your relationship with Jesus, his Father, and his Holy Spirit.

You can foster your growing relationship with Christ by setting aside time each day to pray. All relationships take time and effort to develop—this relationship is no different. You may have to adjust your schedule to find time for prayer, reading, and meditation. It may mean rising earlier, devoting part of a lunch hour, or sacrificing a television program.

Choose a comfortable space for prayer—a quiet corner of a room, a favorite chair, or a place where you can view nature. Even your computer can help stimulate your prayer life. Many websites offer daily prayers and meditations (mission.liguori. org, sacredspace.ie, or loyolapress.com). Setting aside time each day to praise and thank God, to pray petitions, and to listen and seek forgiveness will reinforce prayer as a staple of your life as a Christian leader. You are too busy not to pray.

READ AND STUDY SCRIPTURE

The Scriptures provide inspiration, information, consolation, and grounding. When you read, meditate, and study the Scriptures with openness to the Holy Spirit, the Word of God will speak in your heart. Consider reading a short Scripture passage each day, preparing the Sunday readings ahead of time, or meditating on the daily liturgical readings. Take advantage of one of the many tools available to deepen your knowledge of the Scriptures:

+ Catholic Scripture-study programs such as the Little Rock Scripture Study or Threshold Bible Study

+ Booklets with liturgical readings for each day

+ Websites with daily Scripture reflections(usccb.org) or sites that offer reflection questions on the Sunday readings (wholecommunitycatechesis.com). The USCCB website (usccb.org) includes the revised edition of the *New American Bible*, the daily readings, and podcasts.

FIND INSPIRATION IN SPIRITUAL WRITINGS

Embracing the wisdom found in spiritual mentors can also strengthen your spiritual growth. Uncover insights into the joys, motivation, difficulties, and hard work involved in living a life of Christian discipleship by reading the biographies or writings of holy people such as Francis of Assisi, Teresa of Ávila, Alphonsus Liguori, Ignatius of Loyola, Catherine of Siena, Edith Stein, Mother Teresa, and Pope John XXIII. Find encouragement from modern spiritual leaders such as Henri Nouwen, Joyce Rupp, and Ronald Rolheiser.

ATTEND TO YOUR OWN FORMATION AND EDUCATION

If, as with many Catholics, your formation ended with elementary school religion or confirmation preparation, you'll want to update your understanding of the basic teachings of the Church and your area of ministry through courses, DVDs, or reading.

One of the publications in Liguori's *Handbook* series, *Handbook for Today's Catholic,* offers the fundamentals of Catholicism in a condensed format (liguori.org).

Diocesan classes on doctrine and ministerial methods and your parish adult-enrichment sessions will enhance your formation. Many dioceses and Catholic universities offer certificate programs and online courses for ministry formation.

Catholic periodicals such as *Catholic Digest, Liguorian,* and *St. Anthony Messenger* are inspirational and easy-to-understand sources.

MAINTAIN BALANCE

It's important for leaders to take care of themselves. If stresses or tensions creep into your ministry or if you're walking through difficulties in your personal or spiritual life, allow others to minister to you.

Seek spiritual support from others walking the same journey. Ask for spiritual direction from a person who is more experienced than you in living the spiritual life. A spiritual director will help you uncover the sacred in your life and suggest ways for you to grow in holiness. You can also find support with a small group of spiritual friends who pray together, share faith stories, and nourish each other through regular gatherings.

Your Spiritual Life Cycle

The spiritual life is full of ups and downs, times when you see great progress and times when you wonder if you've progressed at all. It may be helpful to see your spirituality reflected in the liturgical cycle:

+ Advent times, when you prepare and anticipate the Lord in your life

+ Christmas times, when you give birth to Christ in the lives of others

+ Lenten times, which are dry, arid, and soul-searching and you may not feel God's presence at all

+ Easter times, when you experience little deaths leading to new life

+ Pentecost times, when you're energized with the fire of the Holy Spirit

+ Ordinary Times, when you go about your daily work

It's unlikely that these periods in your spiritual life will match the Church's celebration of them. But wherever you are along the path, you have the underlying assurance that the Lord is walking with you.

Well-Grounded Spirituality

As leaders, your spirituality is grounded in a humility modeled most concretely by Mary, the Mother of God. Mary allowed herself to be used as a willing instrument. In a spirit of humility, she gave her *yes* before she understood its implications.

Humility doesn't mean that you belittle or demean yourself, but rather that you have a good sense of your ability. The root word for *humility* is *humus*, the rich soil is derived from decayed organisms in which plants thrive. Humility allows you to know who you really are—a graced yet imperfect individual, a cracked pot nevertheless chosen to go forth and make a difference.

Practical Suggestions for Individuals

◆ Make a commitment to pray each day, just fifteen minutes at first. Mark the time in your calendar or set your alarm.

◆ Use a Bible you can mark up. The *New American Bible, Revised Edition,* is the translation the United States Church uses for liturgy. Begin by reading a small portion of one Gospel. Reread it slowly, and if a word or phrase strikes you, underline it. Stay with that word or phrase, then write it down and keep it as your phrase for the day.

◆ Examine your formation. Even if you have an advanced degree, you can still find places to grow. Write down one or two concrete steps you will take to enhance your formation.

Practical Suggestions for Parish Groups

◆ Consider a study of the *United States Catholic Catechism for Adults*. Begin with one of the prayers or meditation for each chapter and discuss the chapter content using the questions that are provided.

◆ Discuss the value for your parish of putting a question of the week about the Sunday readings in the bulletin. The question can be used in homilies and for brief faith-sharing at the beginning of every parish meeting or class that week. Some religious publishers include questions in English and Spanish on their websites (osvcurriculum.com/lifelong_catechesis/adults.jsp or faithfirst.com/question_week.html).

DEVELOPING PRACTICAL LEADERSHIP SKILLS

This section suggests ways to refine leadership skills and strengthen your parish. Individuals or groups should review the suggestions to determine which can be integrated into their ministries and programs.

7

WORDS HAVE POWER

Remember the Telephone Game? In a large circle, one person whispers a sentence quickly to the next person, who whispers it to the next, and so on around the circle. The last person to hear the message announces the sentence to the entire group. The last sentence spoken is usually very different from the original message.

This entertaining game has a serious message: communications can be heard, understood, and interpreted as the speaker intended, or they can be misheard or misinterpreted. It's especially important to remember this message in the parish setting, where on any given day numerous leaders come together to share information, exchange ideas, make suggestions, develop plans, or express feelings and emotions about a given situation.

People spend a great deal of their lives communicating—sharing ideas and information through speaking, listening, writing and reading. Most people give little thought to the power of their words. Words can instruct, build up, encourage, demonstrate love, and offer support. Words can also discourage, antagonize, tear down, or hurt. As a parish leader, you want to be conscious of the power of words and how communication cues can influence what your listeners hear. Strengthen your awareness of communication methods and how to use them effectively.

How You Communicate

You have countless opportunities to hone your communication skills and techniques as a parish leader. Some of your communicating may take place at the parish, such as at a council meeting, a liturgy-planning session, or a meeting of the finance committee. You may speak before a large group teaching religion, presenting a workshop on liturgy, or giving information on the parish picnic. You may be involved in a small-group discussion such as a Scripture-sharing or bereavement group. Perhaps you'll communicate one-on-one, inviting prospective committee members, asking for donations, or welcoming new parishioners.

Effective leaders understand that true communication isn't one-sided. Good communication involves speaking, listening, and responding. Your communication can provide information, ideas, inspiration, or encouragement to move a project forward. If you're enthusiastic about a project, your excitement will be contagious.

Your communication skills are important tools for initiating, developing, and sustaining effective relationships at your parish. Here are some general ways to refine those skills:

◆ Be genuine and authentic in your speaking and listening. Share your ideas and be honest about your feelings and needs. Allow others to give their input in an atmosphere of acceptance and sensitivity.

◆ Use words that demonstrate courtesy and respect for individuals and their opinions. Well-chosen words promote caring, empathy, and compassion. Avoid offensive language, and don't use slang or clichés that may be misunderstood (especially by those whose first language isn't English).

◆ Listen attentively to further your own knowledge and understanding of others' ideas and beliefs. Paying close attention to what others say and clarifying what they mean lets others know that what they say is important.

◆ Avoid angry speech or words and attitudes that stir up dissension. Don't use language that forces people to choose sides, but rather strive for understanding and consensus. Don't allow gossip or put-downs to infiltrate a conversation or take over a meeting.

◆ Give others an opportunity to think about what is being said. Some people need time to process information. Silence offers an opportunity for people to ponder and weigh what they just heard.

◆ Remember, it's difficult to listen and speak at the same time. Don't prepare your response while another person speaks. Avoid interrupting the speaker. Listen for the speaker's main points to determine what the speaker is expressing.

◆ Use appropriate and nonjudgmental questioning to clarify another person's perspectives or suggestions. Try to summarize what you've heard to be sure it's the intended message.

◆ Don't be critical of people whose viewpoints are different from yours. React to the message, not the person. If you disagree, say so and be clear about your reasons.

◆ Avoid distractions. Turn off your cell phone.

- ♦ Engage in private conversations or important communications in a setting where interruptions will be minimal.

- ♦ When you speak to a group, use notes to be sure to include all your points. Speak slowly and distinctly, and vary your tone of voice.

- ♦ Use a microphone if you're speaking in a large room. If possible, don't stay glued to a podium.

- ♦ Use only the amount of words necessary to make your point. Saying the same thing over and over or saying it louder and louder doesn't mean you're saying it better and better.

COMMUNICATION CUES

In addition to conscious ways of communicating with others, your unconscious communication cues (tone of voice, body language, breathing) can have a great impact on what you say or on what is heard.

Be aware of these additional ways of communicating:

+ Like it or not, the way you present yourself in the first few moments of an encounter affects the message your audience hears. Many public speakers use the first moments of a presentation to tell a joke or a story. They understand that the audience is not really listening to them so much as sizing them up. People pay attention to your facial expressions, gestures, and clothes. A warm and gracious smile, even if the topic is heavy or sad, immediately puts others at ease. A gentle handshake if you're speaking to one person or stepping aside from a podium if you're speaking to a group demonstrates your desire to be one with them. Neat and appropriate dress tells your audience (one person or many) that they're important and that you took time to prepare for your meeting. It's not necessary to wear business attire to a parish meeting or appointment, but neither is it appropriate to wear sweatpants or jogging shorts unless you're a coach.

+ The way you carry your body speaks volumes to your listeners. When you're meeting with one person, standing or leaning over the person can denote a sense of superiority, domination, or authority. Leaning back or moving your chair away from a meeting table can say that you're disinterested and don't take the topic seriously. A roomful of people with crossed arms and legs can mean the group is closed to your ideas. (It can also mean they're cold.) A gentle touch speaks of understanding and concern, but be careful not to invade personal space.

+ When meeting with one person, moderate eye contact says you're interested in what the person is saying. You don't want to stare the person down, so intermittent eye contact is best. Keep in mind that people may avoid eye contact when a topic is uncomfortable and that some people may look past you when they're contemplating your words. If you're speaking to a group, look around the room instead of focusing on one or two people. Also be aware of the cultural sensitivities—in some cultures, direct eye contact is viewed as invasive, rude, or disrespectful.

+ Your pitch or inflection also speaks to the hearer. Your tone of voice can denote emphasis or reveal emotion. It can demonstrate understanding and sympathy or anger or sarcasm. The same words said with different emphases can mean very different things. Depending on the tone of voice, "I want to see you after the meeting" can mean "Let's go out for coffee" or "I need to speak to you in private." A very high-pitched voice and rapid breathing can mean you're nervous; a loud sigh lets everyone know you've had enough of this discussion even if they haven't. When you're speaking, prevent misunderstanding by choosing carefully how you'll say something. If you're nervous about speaking to a person or group, take a deep, cleansing breath before you begin.

+ People like to designate their space. Each week at Mass, people tend to sit in the same pews. If you teach a class or work with a small group, invariably people sit in the same place next to the same people and mark off their space with a coffee cup, notebook, and pen. If you facilitate a group for a period of time, rearrange the room once in a while to give people a different perspective. If you have an office, try to set up a space where you can gather without barriers such as a desk or a table.

THE WRITTEN WORD

As a parish leader, you may be asked to submit announcements or articles for the bulletin or newsletter, prepare flyers for an event, or compose letters to parishioners. A written document has an advantage over the spoken word—you're able to review your communication before you send it to be sure you've said everything correctly. Be attentive to these details:

+ Use correct grammar and spelling. Use the spell checker, but bear in mind that it won't catch everything. Be sure names are accurate.

+ Check the date, time, and place. Sometimes leaders revise a letter or document from a previous year and forget to change the dates or times. Use a calendar to ensure accuracy.

+ Review a document before you send or submit it. Ask someone else to check it before you send it.

+ Keep bulletin announcements brief. Begin with a catch phrase to entice people to read further, but keep it simple and avoid being too cutesy and losing the message.

+ Create a flyer or registration form that includes all pertinent information to avoid needless phone calls to the parish. Include the following information:

  - *Parish name and address at the top of the flyer*
  - *Topic, brief description, and audience (all parishioners, parents of first communicants, people who wish to know more about the Catholic faith)*
  - *Speaker and brief biography*
  - *Time, date, place*
  - *Cost and methods of payment (cash, check, charge) and what the cost includes (materials, refreshments, lunch)*
  - *Ways to register (drop in the collection basket, register at the door, send registration to the parish)*
  - *What participants need to bring (Bible, child's baptismal certificate)*
  - *Name, e-mail, and phone number of contact person*
  - *Additional information (child care, transportation)*

Using Social Media

Communication with hundreds of friends is possible with the press of the send key. Conversely, words you intended for one person can be forwarded to countless others in a flash. Your communication can be archived for future reference. Here are suggestions for using social media:

+ Use e-mails, text messages, and the parish website to announce meetings, remind about upcoming events, and respond to other e-mail or texts. Keep your language simple. As with all written communication, remember that the recipient doesn't have the benefit of the communication cues I mentioned earlier.

+ Always use the subject line in e-mails, and don't reply to all unless specifically asked to do so.

+ Avoid using the parish computer for personal communication.

+ Do not use e-mail to respond to a person's private concerns, give advice, or respond to an emotionally hot topic. E-mails are not confidential documents and, like all written communications, are subject to misinterpretation. Use an in-person meeting or phone call to discuss personal or confidential matters.

+ Avoid using e-mail to dash off an angry response or to say something you don't want to say in person. If the potential exists for embarrassment, harm, or misinterpretation, don't send the message.

+ Get parental permission to e-mail minors or if you're asking minors to use the Internet.

+ Be thoughtful and prudent about what you post on social-networking sites. Avoid posts you wouldn't want to be seen by the parish staff, parents, youth, or other parishioners.

+ Use the parish website and social-networking sites to publicize upcoming events or to display photos or videos of parish programs. Get parent permission before you post images of people under age eighteen. Follow all parish webmaster and diocesan guidelines.

CHOOSE YOUR WORDS WELL

Words have great power. In the beginning when God spoke, order emerged from chaos, light separated from darkness, and humans populated the Earth (Genesis 1). Ultimately when God spoke the Word, the Word was made flesh, dwelt among humans and brought salvation (Nicene Creed).

As a parish leader, your words have power. Your words, whether spoken or unspoken, can cement or deter relationships. Kind words can invite and include, while argumentative or insensitive words can discourage and exclude. Your words can be understood and appreciated, or they can be misinterpreted or misunderstood and undermine your work as a leader. Your words have great power. Choose them well.

8

MEETINGS, MEETINGS, MEETINGS

It's undeniable that meetings are an important fact of parish life. When you plan a meeting, be sure it's worth the time and energy of the attendees. Conduct meetings that achieve goals, move projects ahead, encourage continued participation, foster community, strengthen parish life, and further the parish mission and vision. Every parish meeting—even business meetings—should have as its underlying goals the growth, development, and maturity of the people of God.

ALL MEETINGS

+ Ensure the meeting's purpose and expected outcomes are clear to the participants.

+ Send the agenda and pertinent materials to participants three to five days ahead of time and urge them to review it and collect any other data they will need. Remind them that the success of the meeting doesn't depend only on those in charge of the meeting.

+ Follow the agenda. Schedule the meeting for about one and one-half to two hours, and begin and end on time.

Place important decision items early on the agenda. Too often the majority of a meeting is spent discussing reports, and then important items such as funding an adult-formation program or beginning a preschool are decided when people are tired and want to go home.

+ Don't schedule meetings that conflict with parish or community events that are important to a large number of people. A sacramental-preparation program for parents scheduled on Super Bowl Sunday is almost always doomed to fail.

+ Don't hold an unnecessary meeting. If the agenda has no discussion items, simply send reports or information to the participants.

+ Prepare a comfortable setting. Make sure the room isn't too hot or cold. Use appropriate liturgical colors and set out a Bible and candles. These visual symbols set a spiritual tone that reminds participants that the underlying purpose of all parish meetings is to build up the Body of Christ. Light refreshments speak of warmth and hospitality and allow social interaction aside from the agenda. For discussion, seat people around a table or in a circle so they can see each other. For presentations, arrange the room theater-style, ensuring that participants can see the speaker and any media. If participants will have materials, use tables and be sure everyone has a sightline to the speaker. Use a microphone in a large room to ensure that everyone can hear.

+ Begin meetings with prayer. For one-time meetings, a short Scripture reading and summary prayer is fine. Groups that meet regularly can use a brief prayer with time for faith-sharing to help participants grow together spiritually. A Question of the Week format, discussed at the end of Chapter 6, provides a suitable format for prayer and sharing.

+ Be prepared. Have easy access to paper, pencils, stapler, tape, paper clips, scissors, an extension cord, a power strip and, for evening meetings, a flashlight.

+ Check all media before the meeting. Set up computers, PowerPoint presentations, and CD or DVD players ahead of time to be sure they are in good working order.

+ Have access to a phone, emergency numbers, and a first-aid kit. Be aware of emergency procedures and exit routes.

+ Manage your time well. Allow time for people to socialize and exchange ideas. If people will meet on a regular basis, use a simple exercise for introductions. Have participants state their names, perhaps their occupations, and the reason for choosing this committee or what they hope to receive from this program.

+ Do not allow one person to dominate a meeting with endless repetition. A good way to stop someone who is monopolizing a discussion is to say, "Thank you for your input. Does anyone else have any input?

+ If the discussion gets too emotional, intense, or angry, call for quiet time so people can calm down and rethink the topic. Ensure that all participants have the opportunity to state their input in a nonthreatening atmosphere. Give each person two or three minutes to express his or her opinion without interruption. Determine whether a consensus can be reached. If not, the topic may need to be tabled for further study, reflection, and discussion. Perhaps the situation necessitates giving all the information and discussion points to the pastor or a staff member for resolution.

+ Avoid meetings-after-the-meeting in the parking lot. These impromptu gatherings are divisive and encourage people to choose sides. Before the meeting ends, ask for a spirit of solidarity. Foster an understanding that while everyone in attendance wants what is best for the parish, there is currently disagreement about which option is best. Making a decision everyone can support may mean that at the next meeting participants have to weigh the pros and cons of the options and give in a little so they can come to a consensus.

SMALL GROUPS

+ Set the tone by explaining the format and structure of the sessions and providing an overview of the materials.

+ Review questions or concerns from the last gathering.

+ Lead a discussion of new material by inviting participants to surface key points, respond to questions provided in materials, and share applications.

+ End sessions with a brief summary and a review of assignment for next session.

HOSTING SPEAKERS

+ Follow parish and diocesan guidelines for using outside

presenters. Get approval for the speaker and topic before you invite the speaker.

+ Work out all financial arrangements in advance. In addition to a stipend, out-of-town speakers usually require travel expenses, housing, and meals. Send the speaker written confirmation of the date, length of presentation, place, topic, and financial and other arrangements.

+ Ask the speaker to send a brief topic description and biography to be used for publicity.

+ Ask the speaker what equipment, handouts, or other materials will be needed.

+ Touch base with the speaker a couple of weeks before the presentation to confirm arrangements and answer any questions. Review driving directions or let the speaker know who will meet him or her at the airport.

+ Determine whether the speaker is open to answering questions. Some presenters prefer to have questions submitted in writing. This allows a presenter to group similar questions for one response.

+ Request the stipend from the parish office ahead of time so you can compensate the speaker in a timely manner.

+ Ask a trusted parishioner to welcome the speaker and help him or her set up if you will be busy with other details.

+ Set up and check all equipment ahead of time to ensure it's in working order. Provide a podium and a glass of water.

+ Be sure the people who register the participants are aware of their responsibilities. If they're collecting fees, they need a cash box with small bills for change. They should also know whom checks should be made out to and how to handle credit card transactions.

+ Begin on time with prayer and introductions. The introduction should not be too lengthy, but should summarize the speaker's major accomplishments and convey warmth and welcome to the speaker and participants.

+ Ask whether the speaker would like to be notified when time is almost up. End the session on time with a few words of summary and appreciation.

+ Send a formal thank you note to the presenter within a couple of days of the presentation.

9

VISION AND
PROGRAM PLANNING

Many vibrant parishes have created their own vision statements, specific declarations of how they will carry out the mission of Christ. A vision statement is succinct and inspiring. It expresses the spiritual purpose of a parish, why this particular parish exists, and what this parish calls its members to do.

A vision statement can be developed using a simple process facilitated by a parish-leadership team that includes the pastor and parish staff. The process should involve between thirty and forty parishioners who reflect the make-up of the parish. Here are some concrete steps to developing a vision statement:

+ Pray for the inspiration of the Holy Spirit.

+ Identify and list the parish's ministries, activities, and programs. Group similar activities.

+ Reflect on these groupings. Why do these activities exist? What beliefs or convictions motivate the parish to initiate and support them? How are they related to the Gospel message and the fundamental beliefs of the faith?

+ Analyze the similarities and differences between programs. Reach a consensus about what best reflects the unique character of the parish.

+ Use small groups to develop draft statements that reflect why this parish exists and what it calls parish members to do. Bring the statements back to the entire group for discussion. Choose one statement or combine elements of several statements. The leadership team polishes and refines the statement. The pastor and parish council affirm the statement.

+ Make the statement available in church, the bulletin, and on the parish website.

+ Announce the vision statement to the parish in a celebratory manner.

+ Ensure that all future planning and new programming contribute to fulfilling the vision of the parish.

PLANNING EFFECTIVE PROGRAMS

Parishes fulfill their vision by developing and maintaining programs that nourish, strengthen, and encourage their members. Dynamic parishes thrive on programming that occurs at all times of the day and evening. As you plan or initiate a program, consider how it will advance parish vision. Here are some helps for initiating a new program or refreshing an existing one:

+ Get approval for the program concept.

+ Form a team or committee of parishioners interested in the program or activity. Include those with expertise in the field and representatives of the people most affected by the program. Keep the pastor or appropriate staff person informed of your progress. Each time you meet, pray for the inspiration of the Holy Spirit.

+ Determine and list the goals and objectives of the program. What do you hope to accomplish? Who are the recipients? What strategies will you use to accomplish your objectives?

+ Research existing programs by studying written material, examining packaged programs, visiting parishes with similar programs, and meeting with those who have expertise or experience.

+ Use the data to determine the general framework of the program. If necessary, adjust the goals, objectives, and strategies.

+ Map out the details of the program. What will it look like? When will it begin? Who is needed? What materials are needed? Where will the program occur?

+ Set a timeline by working backward from the program launch date to determine when tasks need to be done and who will do them.

+ Establish a budget, including estimated income as well as expenditures.

+ Get approval for the program before you begin. If several people or groups need to approve the program, it may stretch your time frame.

+ Reserve space and secure speakers and workers.

FINANCIAL ACCOUNTABILITY

Very few parish programs can be maintained without financial support. As a leader, be certain you're accountable for all finances you handle. Different dioceses and pastors have different ways of dealing with money: one pastor may tell you to request what you need directly from him or the parish secretary. Another may suggest you set up a checking account in the name of the program or group. Others will give you a petty-cash account or ask you to lay out your own money and be reimbursed. Sometimes the parish subsidizes all or part of the program; sometimes the program is financed through registration fees or a benefactor (sometimes a parish organization). Some pastors may ask you to submit a complete program budget before a program is approved.

No matter what, always keep accurate, detailed records of all financial transactions. If your parish doesn't have a specific budget process, the following points will help you be accountable:

+ Set up a simple budget by determining your income and expenditures (income = any anticipated fees, subsidies, or sponsorship money; expenditures = costs such as books or materials, speaker fees and expense, office supplies, printing, mailing, and refreshments).

+ Keep an uncomplicated ledger with columns for income and expenditures. Each time you take in money, record the date, amount, name, and type of payment. Each time you spend money, record the date, amount, and reason. Use simple spreadsheet software. Always get and keep receipts.

+ Count the money before you turn it in. Write a short summary memo stating the total amount in cash and checks and the name of your program. Keep a copy of the memo for your records.

+ When requesting reimbursement, submit a short memo with the amount and your name. Attach all receipts and keep a copy.

VISION INVOLVES CHANGE

As a parish leader involved in the planning or coordinating of programs, you can expect some obstacles. Very few parishes want to initiate several new programs at the same time. Few finance committees like to approve new expenditures. New ideas, new programs, and new ways of thinking require someone or something to change.

No matter what the change—a new system to clear the parking lot after Mass, a new method of raising finances, new liturgical norms—someone is likely to disagree. You'll hear statements like, "Our parish isn't ready for this," "It costs too much," "People won't like it," "We're all too busy for that." Remember that people often react negatively to change because they fear leaving what is comfortable, they're protecting their turf, or they're complacent and don't want to do anything differently.

Be prepared to support your vision, idea or program with data, examples, demonstrations, and even professional expertise. Change may take time and be difficult, but living entities must grow and change. Only change can bring about conversion and transformation.

10

PEOPLE—THE MOST IMPORTANT RESOURCE

The most important resource of any parish is its people. It is the task of every staff member and parish leader to invite, empower, and mentor fresh leaders. These emerging leaders are so much more than volunteers. They are new disciples responding to their baptismal call to carry on the work of Christ.

Parish leaders are priceless commodities. Parishes should spend time and resources recruiting, training, managing, and nourishing their current, new, and future leaders—the return on this investment reaps many benefits.

Motivation

People respond to the call to serve for many reasons. Capitalize on these reasons when recruiting and mentoring others. People respond to the call to serve because they

+ are dedicated to serving others and want to live Gospel values in a concrete way;

+ are grateful to God and want to give back to the Church;

+ have unique skills and aptitudes to put at the service of the Lord;

+ have found time to do a little more for the Church;

+ want to meet others who share the same faith and beliefs;

+ believe in a cause; and

+ see an opportunity to exercise power and influence.

When preparing bulletin announcements or asking people to serve, include these reasons in your recruiting efforts: "If you want to make a difference in parish life…," or "This would be a great opportunity to practice the works of mercy," or "This is a wonderful way to meet other parents of tweens and teens." These statements will appeal to people who are service oriented, who want to assert influence, or who would like to meet other parishioners. A personal invitation to someone who has a beautiful singing voice may encourage that person to become a cantor and serve in a way he or she had never considered.

Keep in mind that people will respond positively most often when they receive a personal invitation from another leader or when they know the person who invites them. As a parish leader, consider recruitment of new leaders as one of your ongoing, year-round tasks. Be on the lookout for people who will be a good match for *any* parish program, not just yours. If you encounter someone whose gifts and talents are better suited to another ministry, guide the person in that direction and inform that program leader about your discovery.

RECRUITMENT

It's challenging to recruit parish leaders. Remember that you're inviting people to participate in the work of Christ and his Church. Be positive and proud of your part in recruiting disciples. Here are some suggestions:

+ Pray for guidance from the Holy Spirit in making decisions.

+ Present the task as worthwhile: Saying the task won't take much time, or that anybody can do it, or that there is really nothing to it can belittle the service. No one wants to do a task that isn't valuable, effective, or meaningful. Tell the person how this service will contribute to the mission of the Church.

+ Prepare a brief job description, including major tasks, responsibilities, reporting structure, and training.

+ Break large tasks into smaller parts. You may find that a person is a great match for a program or activity but cannot commit the time necessary. Consider dividing the service into smaller time segments. Often the person will know someone who can share the tasks.

+ Participate in a ministry of presence. Be available after Sunday Masses and at social times. Get to know the parishioners.

+ Be sure to follow through with people who sign up. After a parish-ministry fair, an announcement calling for people to serve, or a Service-Pledge Sunday, make timely contact with those who respond. If you already have enough people, suggest another way for people to serve. It's discouraging to sign up and not be contacted.

+ Consult with key leadership. Advise the priests and deacons, parish secretary, parish-council members, and other leaders about the people you need for your program. Involve all parish leadership in recruitment, and give them a stake in what you're doing.

+ From time to time publish a wish list of people you need for a program or a one-time event. A creative list could include photographers, cookie bakers, greeters, crafters, and people to send thank you notes. Publicize your wish list in the parish bulletin, with other parish groups, and on the parish website, social-networking sites, and bulletin boards. Be sure to specify tasks people can do at home.

+ Tap all ages and groups. Invite senior citizens, youth, young adults, and young married couples—sometimes they have more time and fewer family commitments. Advise parish cultural groups and renewal groups about the program—often they're looking for outreach activities.

+ Use an interest-finder form. Have new parishioners complete a form listing their talents, interests, hobbies, and experience. Include a place for "no experience, but willing to learn." Remember to contact these people.

+ Accept refusals gracefully. When a person is unable to serve, always express gratitude for their time in listening to your request. Graciously leave the door open for next time.

Parish Responsibility

The parish staff and leaders have obligations to people who respond to the call to serve:

+ Interview and place people in suitable positions, matching their gifts, talents, and desires with areas of service.

+ Set a time of service so no one feels locked into a ministry for life.

+ Encourage orientation to new ministry through parish-sponsored formation courses, workshops, or one-on-one meetings.

+ Supervise parishioners in leadership positions. Show an interest in problems and take steps to correct them.

+ Supply materials at the expense of the parish. No one should personally have to bear the cost of all or part of a program unless they choose to make this type of contribution. At minimum, there should be a system of reimbursement.

+ Provide resources such as written and media materials, printing, and equipment.

+ Keep accurate records of service.

+ Provide childcare or transportation.

+ Offer opportunities for fellowship such as socials, retreats, and reflection days. Involve new leaders in planning and evaluating programs.

+ Recognize service through commitment ceremonies, blessings, and acknowledgements in the bulletin using other parish and diocesan communication tools.

+ Show appreciation to leaders and their families with end-of-year gatherings, thank you notes, and surprises.

EVALUATION OF SERVICE

It's helpful to conduct an evaluation of service as people complete projects or programs. This helps improve the program and refines recruitment and mentoring methods. Here are some questions for evaluation and future planning; add others specific to the program.

+ Was this ministry or service what you expected it to be?

+ Did you feel prepared for your work? If not, what would have made you feel more prepared?

+ How were you supported in your work?

+ How can this program or activity be improved?

+ Are you interested in continuing in this service?

+ Are you interested in another ministry?

Collaboration

The parish community has no room for lone rangers. A collaborative working relationship among parish staff and other parish leaders is crucial to the Church's mission and the parish's vision. Parish leaders should strive for maturity and a collaborative effort that allows them to sustain friendships, acknowledge and affirm other people, and express dissatisfaction appropriately.

The letters of Saint Paul and the Acts of the Apostles make it clear that the early Church envisioned all Christians working together to spread the Gospel. Paul mentions many men and women who were his collaborators and partners in ministry, including the deaconess Phoebe (Romans 16:1–2), Prisca and Aquila (Romans 16:3–4), Timothy (Romans 16:21), and Philemon and Apphia (Philemon, verse 2). The Acts of the Apostles details stories of collaboration and fellowship as the Church selects a replacement for Judas (1:15–26), devotes itself to communal living (2:42–47), and meets in house churches like the ones hosted by Lydia (16:40) and Mary the mother of John (12:12–17).

The ministers and ministries Paul refers to include apostles, prophets, preachers, teachers, healers, evangelists, pastors, those who speak in tongues, and those who interpret tongues (1 Corinthians 12; Ephesians 4:11). The abundance of gifts and fruits poured out by the Holy Spirit include knowledge, faith, healing, miraculous powers, discernment of spirits, signs and wonders (1 Corinthians 12:4–11; Hebrews 2:4). No one person had all the gifts. No one could single-handedly carry out the mission. All the gifts and ministries were important and necessary (1 Corinthians 12:12–31).

The ministries and gifts showered on the early Church were meant to complement each other, to unify the community, and to build up of the body of Christ (Ephesians 4:3–13). Today collaborative leaders strive to foster this same unity and communion. Grateful for the many gifts bestowed on the Church, collaborative leaders are not threatened by working with other gifted and talented leaders.

Some leaders view themselves as bosses who make all decisions, experts who have all the answers, or achievers who single-handedly complete all the tasks. But many strive to be collaborative leaders, accomplishing goals and achieving the vision by working with and through other people. Collaborative leaders empower others to succeed by mentoring, modeling, and accompanying others through success, difficulty, or even failure. These leaders apprentice neophytes, pair the right people with the proper tasks, and offer constructive suggestions. Collaborative leaders want others to thrive and provide support, information, recognition, and training to that end.

Collaboration is not easy. It means relinquishing the "I" and "mine" mentality, opting instead for an "ours" perspective. Collaborative leader don't use phrases like "my program," "my equipment," or "my meeting." Pride or arrogance and gossip, rumor, and innuendo have no place. Collaboration requires give and take and working together with different personality types. Collaboration means letting go of one's own ideas and embracing those of others when the good of the parish demands it.

CONFIDENTIALITY

You may encounter people who share delicate, personal, or private information with you. You may be privy to sensitive discussions at staff meetings or at parish gatherings. People who open themselves to you need an atmosphere of trust. Leaders hold in confidence the words, situations, or experiences shared in a private setting and don't disclose them without permission unless the well-being of the person demands it.

Leading others takes time, talent, and effort. Most of all, it takes a Christ-centered approach to people who need you to be there for them.

11

PERSEVERING
AS A LEADER

In saying yes to a leadership role in the Church, you pledge to use your gifts, talents, time, and energy to spread the Gospel. Your yes carries many responsibilities. Sometimes you'll wonder, *Why did I ever say yes?* Other times, you'll want to say, *Use someone else, Lord, because I'm overwhelmed and underappreciated.* Still other times, you'll ask, *Did you really want me, Lord?*

Leaders often take very good care of others and pay little attention to themselves. But you need to keep physically, emotionally, psychologically, and spiritually healthy. Remember, you can't give what you don't have. Here are some tips:

+ Pay attention to diet, exercise, and sleep so you're physically strong and mentally acute.

+ Counteract energy drains with activities that reenergize. If lengthy meetings sap you, unwind with a craft or hobby. If you're stressed by conflicts in a relationship, have a cup of tea with a special friend. If a messy office overwhelms you, organize your space.

+ If you have difficulty with time management, keep a time log for a week. Determine what activities are essential and important, what can be delegated, and what can be left undone.

+ Use a scheduling application to remind you of daily, weekly, monthly, and yearly tasks. Allow substantial blocks of uninterrupted time for planning. Create to-do lists each day. As you complete tasks and meet deadlines, reward yourself with a walk around the parish grounds or have lunch with a friend.

+ Set flexible priorities. When you work in the Church, pastoral circumstances often change your schedule. Remember, people are always more important than programs or activities. Sometimes interruptions are where real ministry happens.

+ Move on at the right time. If you've outgrown a program or ministry, if your service no longer brings you joy, or if other commitments demand a change, move on with grace and dignity.

+ Persevere in leadership. Even when you say no to one commitment, as a Christian leader you will continue to serve the Lord. Spend time with a spiritual friend or spiritual director to discern where the Lord is leading you next.

Concluding Remarks
From a Well-Aged ULP

When I was new to Church leadership, a very dear nun told me something that has guided my entire ministry. I saw that she and our parish priest were bringing many people to a committed life in the Lord. I was awed and overwhelmed by the way they had dedicated their lives to spreading the Gospel. I didn't feel productive as a Christian leader—my days were consumed with cooking, cleaning, and laundry for my husband and, at the time, five children.

I expressed my deep frustration to Sister Therese. Her response was loving and lovely, but it pierced me to the core. She said, "Ginger, you are where you are so that Christ might be there."

This statement has become a touchstone for me. I've spent my life and ministry discerning what those words mean for me in any situation.

I invite you to take these words to heart. They say something not only about your role as a leader, but also about your call to discipleship. Wherever you are, at any given moment—at home, at work, at the parish, in your neighborhood—*you are where you are so that Christ might be there.*

It doesn't matter whether you have a title, an office, power, or prestige. You are the leader who can bring Christ to each person, situation, and environment you encounter.

You are the leader who can call forth new disciples.

You are the leader who can influence others to use their gifts to spread the Gospel.

You are the leader who can see in others what they do not see in themselves.

You are the presence of Christ.

References

All websites were accessed August 30, 2011.

Catechism of the Catholic Church, English Translation, Second Edition (CCC). Washington, DC: United States Catholic Conference, 1997. usccb.org

"Called and Gifted for the Third Millennium." Washington, DC: United States Conference of Catholic Bishops, 1995. usccb.org

Code of Canon Law. vatican.va/archive/ENG1104/_INDEX.HTM (case sensitive).

Covey, Stephen. *The Seven Habits of Highly Effective People.* New York: Simon & Schuster, 1989.

Co-Workers in the Vineyard of the Lord. Washington, DC: United States Conference of Catholic Bishops, 2005. usccb.org/about/laity-marriage-family-life-and-youth/laity/

Flannery, Austin, OP (Ed.). *Vatican Council II: The Conciliar and Post Conciliar Documents.* Northport, NY: Costello Publishing Company, 1975.

"Follow the Way of Love." Washington, DC: United States Conference of Catholic Bishops, 1994. usccb.org

Go and Make Disciples. Washington, DC: United States Conference of Catholic Bishops, 2002. usccb.org/beliefs-and-teachings/how-we-teach/evangelization/

Handbook for Today's Catholic. Liguori, MO: Liguori Publications, 2004. liguori.org

Infantino, Ginger. *Handbook for Today's Catechist.* Liguori, MO: Liguori, 2009. liguori.org

National Directory for Catechesis. Washington, DC: United States Conference of Catholic Bishops, 2005.

Pope Benedict XVI. "Church Membership and Pastoral Co-Responsibility," May 26 2009. vatican.va/holy_father/benedict_xvi/, click on "Speeches."

Pope Benedict XVI. "Angelus Message," March 7, 2010. catholicnewsagency.com/news/true_wisdom_needed_to_understand_suffering_holy_father_teaches/

Pope Paul VI. On Evangelization in the Modern World (*Evangelii Nuntiandi*), 1975. vatican.va/holy_father/paul_vi/apost_exhortations/documents/hf_p-vi_exh_19751208_evangelii-nuntiandi_en.html